THE
BIG
BOOK
OF
BEASTS

Words and pictures
YUVAL ZOMMER

Beast expert
BARBARA TAYLOR

Can you find ...
... this mystery paw print
15 times in the book?
Watch out for imposters.

THE
BIG
BOOK
OF
BEASTS

Thames & Hudson

WHO'S INSIDE?

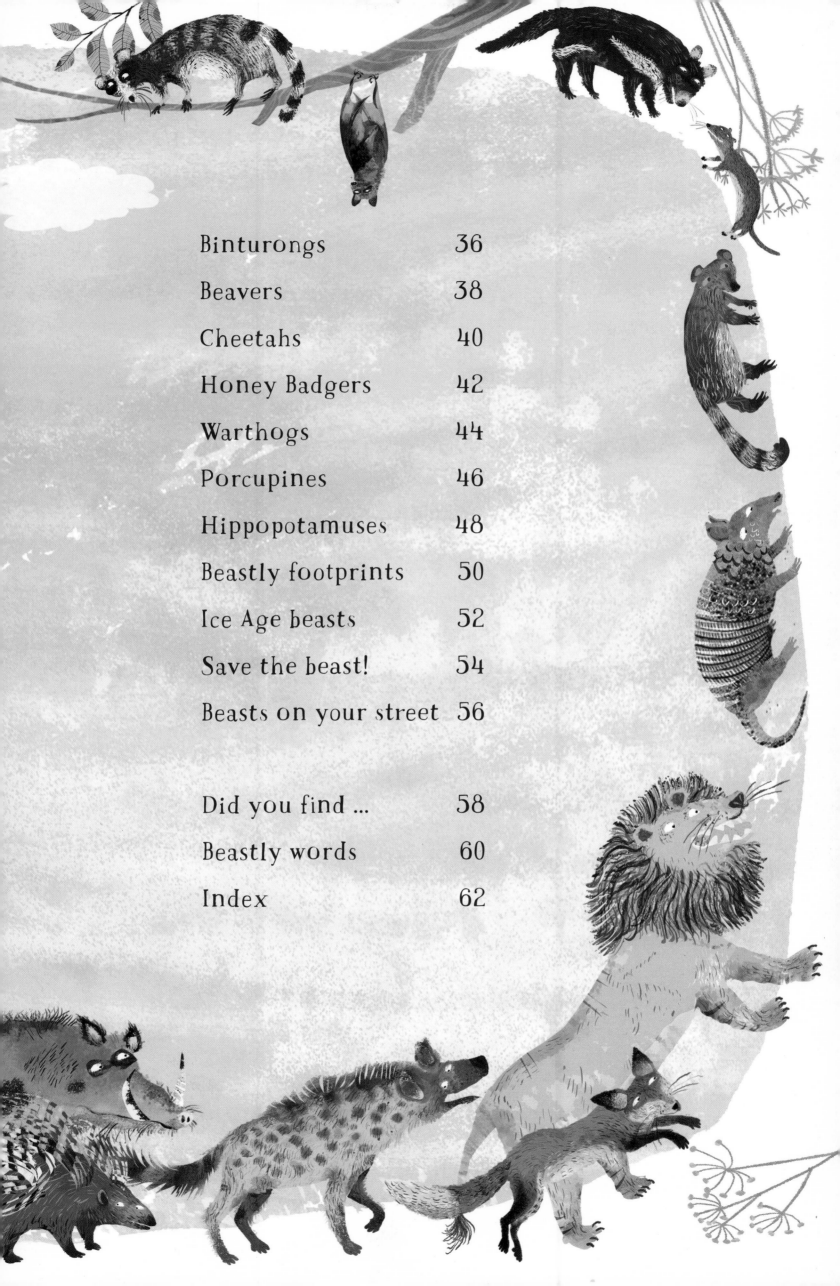

BEASTLY FAMILIES

What makes a mammal a beast?

Warm-blooded animals with hair or fur have the scientific name "mammals." Some mammals are friendly and some are beastly! Beasts are deadly, cunning and most importantly, wild! Here's a who's who of the most beastly of the bunch.

Primates ...
... include monkeys and apes
... eat fruit and insects

Even-toed ungulates ...
... have hooves and an even number of toes
... include warthogs and hippos
... eat plants

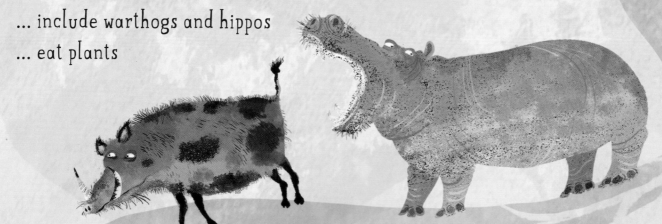

Rodents ...
... have four big front teeth
... include mice and rats as well as beavers and porcupines

Bats ...

... are a family all of their own

... eat fruit and insects

... sometimes just drink blood

... make up a quarter of
all mammals

Carnivores ...

... all eat meat

... include all big cats

... include bears, hyenas, weasels,
binturongs, cheetahs, wolves, foxes
and honey badgers

Armadillos and sloths ...

... are both in the same family called "xenarthra"

... eat plants and insects

... digest things super slowly

Marsupials ...

... include kangaroos and Tasmanian devils

... eat plants

... have pouches to carry their babies in

CLAWS AND JAWS

How does a beast protect itself?

Beasts use their claws and jaws for all sorts of things like hunting, fighting, protecting themselves and sometimes just for showing off. Here are some of the most spectacular and terrifying teeth and talons.

Get a grip!

A cheetah has especially long claws for gripping the ground and a sharp thumb claw to hook its prey.

As tough as nails

An anteater has long, strong claws for ripping open termite mounds that are as hard as concrete.

Handy tools

A mole's claws are shaped just like little shovels. It uses them to burrow through soil and make mole hills.

Vampire teeth

A vampire bat uses its needle-like teeth to cut a 'V' shape into a cow's skin. It licks the blood that comes out using its tiny grooved tongue.

Grizzly gnashers

A brown bear uses its super-strong teeth to crack open bones to get to the juicy marrow inside.

Toothy terror

A hippo lets its mouth gape open so that it can show off its frightening teeth and scare its rivals.

HOWLS, GROWLS AND SMELLS

How does a beast make itself known?

There are lots of ways beasts can give off signs that they are nearby even when you can't see them. Some are smelly, some are loud and some are very surprising!

Roaaaaar!

Lots of big cats roar to make themselves sound scary and keep in touch with each other. A lion has the loudest roar of all.

Porcupine tantrum

A crested porcupine frightens off predators by stamping its feet while grunting and hissing.

Stink bomb

A honey badger produces a stink
bomb to stun its enemies.

The sweet smell of slime

A beaver marks its territory with a thick
slime that smells just like vanilla. It is
even used as a flavoring in food.

Screaming armadillos!

A screaming armadillo screams
at its enemies until they go away.

ARMADILLOS

Why is an armadillo covered in armor?

To protect it from wolves, cougars and other hungry predators! Tough bony plates cover its back, head, legs and tail. Only its tummy is soft.

An armadillo digs burrows

Huge front claws and strong legs help an armadillo to tunnel into the ground.

Armadillos have long, sticky tongues ...

... to lick up ants and other bugs as quickly as possible.

How does it hide its soft tummy?

Most armadillos dig a hole to protect themselves. But the three-banded armadillo can roll itself up into a hard ball.

FOXES

Is a fox clever?

Very, especially when it hunts.
A fox can work out exactly how far
away dinner is, even without seeing it!

The smallest sounds

A fox can hear an earthworm
wriggle across the ground and
a mouse digging under its feet!

A fox curls up to keep warm

When it's cold, a fox wraps itself up
in its big, bushy tail.

SNEAKING AROUND A FOREST IN NORTH AMERICA

It sneaks up on a mouse and pounces

A fox leaps high into the air to strike from above.
It can land right on top of a tiny scurrying mouse.

Extra supplies

If a fox has spare food, it digs a
small hidey-hole to save it for later.

Did you know ...

... that a group of foxes is called a skulk?

15

BABOONS

How grumpy is a baboon?

Baboons are crafty and quarrelsome and get into lots of fights. They are very intelligent and share 91% of their DNA with humans.

Barking baboons

A baboon barks, slaps the ground and grinds its teeth to scare away enemies.

Baboon piggyback

A baby baboon clings to its mother's back for the first few months of its life.

A built-in cushion

A baboon has a cushion-like patch of skin on its behind. This cushion makes such a comfy seat that a baboon sleeps sitting upright.

Baboons make friends ...

... by picking ticks out of each other's fur.

BATS

Are bats really blind?

No! All bats can see but some bats can see better than others. Fruit bats have amazing eyesight which they use to look for food. Insect-eating bats don't have very good eyes. They make high-pitched sounds that bounce off the insects so that they can tell where they are.

Webbed fingers

A bat's wings are made from flaps of skin between its long spindly fingers!

FLITTING THROUGH THE DUSK

Hanging around

A bat sleeps hanging upside-down because its bones aren't strong enough for it to stand up. A bat wraps its wings around itself like a blanket when it sleeps.

Mothers' meeting

Bat moms live together when their babies are young.
All the baby bats look the same but they have different
voices so that the moms can find the right baby.

Vampire bats

A South American vampire bat drinks blood
from cows and pigs. It has special spit that
stops the blood from clotting while it drinks.

19

SLOTHS

Just how lazy is a sloth?

Very! It is the world's slowest-moving animal.
A sloth isn't very energetic because it takes
it a whole month to digest one meal.

Hang about!

A sloth has long claws that it uses like hooks
to hang upside-down from trees. A sloth's insides
are fixed onto its ribs. This stops its lungs from
getting squashed when it hangs upside-down.

Did you know ...

... a sloth can turn its head all the way
around until it's looking over its shoulder.

A sloth can turn green

A sloth moves so slowly, a slimy green layer
that looks like mold starts to grow in its fur.
This helps a sloth to blend into the treetops.

Smell I never

Lots of predators find their prey by following
its scent. A sloth gives off no smell at all to
protect itself from being hunted down.

TIGERS

Why is a tiger stripy?

So it stays hidden when it is hunting for its dinner. No two tiger's stripes are the same.

The biggest cat in the world

A tiger is the biggest, strongest and most powerful cat in the world.

A cat who likes water?!

Tigers are good swimmers and love to cool off in ponds and rivers.

A tiger has healing powers

When a tiger licks a wound, its spit helps to heal its skin.

A mother tiger carries her cubs ...

... in her mouth! When a mother tiger senses danger, she keeps her cubs safe by carrying them by the scruff of their necks.

Did you know ...

... a tiger can weigh as much as ten ten-year-old humans.

WOLVES

Why do wolves howl at the moon?

A wolf howls to keep in touch with its pack.
A wolf can hear howls from miles around.

Glow in the dark

A wolf's eyes have reflective parts
that makes them glow in the dark!

Leaders of the pack

The oldest male and female wolf are in charge of the pack. They show their importance by standing tall and showing their teeth.

Did you know ...

... a wolf can make 17 different facial expressions?

Baby blue eyes

Wolf cubs are born with blue eyes. Their eyes turn yellow when they are 8 months old.

25

BROWN BEARS

Where does a brown bear go in winter?

It sleeps in a warm, dark den. Brown bears find a cave or hollow log to hibernate in until spring.

Bears love honey

They raid beehives and lick up the honey with their long tongue. Brown bears eat the young bees, too!

Did you know ...

... brown bears have fur between their toes?

Alaskan bears feast on salmon

They stand in the water to scoop out the fish with their enormous paws. Sometimes they stand at the top of waterfalls to wait for the fish to leap right into their mouths.

Keep away, I live here!

Brown bears rub against trees or rocks to leave their smell behind. They are telling other bears to keep away.

WEASELS

How crafty is a weasel?

It may be the smallest meat-eating mammal but a weasel is a sneaky, strong and ruthless hunter.

A weasel has a bendy spine

A weasel's bendy spine and slim body mean it can chase prey into underground burrows.

Dinner dance

A weasel hypnotizes its prey by doing a hopping, twisting war dance.

A stoat is just like a weasel ...

... except a stoat has a black spot
on the end of its tail

Jumping weasels

Weasels move by doing small, fast jumps.
They stand upright on their hind legs to
look around and plan where to jump to next.

LIONS

How loud is a lion's roar?

A lion's roar can be heard up to 5 miles away (you could walk for 100 minutes and still hear it!) It is the loudest of any animal in the big cat family.

Friends forever

Lions are the only big cats to live in groups, called prides. They stay friends by licking each other and rubbing heads.

Lions are the laziest big cat

A lion sleeps for 16-20 hours a day, sometimes on its back with its paws in the air. Lions are also known to snooze in trees.

LOUNGING IN A SUB-SAHARAN GRASSLAND

Ladies second

Lionesses are smaller and faster than male lions. They do most of the hunting but males eat first!

Not just for looks

A male lion has a thick mane to make him look more frightening and to protect his neck when fighting.

31

TASMANIAN DEVILS

Is a Tasmanian devil a devil?

You might think so if you heard one at night!
When in danger, a devil flies into a rage and
makes a spine-chilling screech.

The devil's ears

When a devil is excited or upset,
blood flows into its pointy pink
ears and they turn red!

Did you know ...

... that Tasmanian devils
only live in Tasmania?

Baby devils are called imps or joeys

Tasmanian devils are marsupials. This means
that a mother devil carries her baby in a
pouch on her front.

A Tasmanian devil isn't fussy

A devil will happily eat half-rotten animals.
It will even eat the bones and fur!

Their powerful jaws ...

... crunch right through bones.

HYENAS

Do hyenas really laugh?

A hyena talks to its family by shouting and cackling. At night time the noises it makes sound like spooky laughter.

Team work

A hyena lives with up to 80 others in a clan. They always hunt in cunning teams but squabble about sharing the food they catch.

A hyena makes itself look bigger ...

... by making the fur along its spine stand on end.

SKULKING IN THE AFRICAN GRASSLANDS

Can you find ...

... a white hyena poo? A hyena eats every part of an animal – even the bones! This is what turns a hyena's poo white.

The females are in charge

Even as a cub, a female hyena is more muscular and aggressive than a male.

BINTURONGS

Is a binturong a cat or a bear?

Neither! A binturong looks like a cross between a cat and a bear, but they are their own unique beast.

Binturongs live in the tops of trees

A binturong uses its tail like a seat belt to stop it from falling out of trees when sleeping. Its tail has a leathery patch at the tip to give it extra grip.

Binturongs love their greens

Even though binturongs are carnivores, which means they eat meat, they mainly eat fruit as well as leaves and small plants.

Shady character

A binturong's shaggy black fur hides
it at night. It feels its way through
the dark using its long, white whiskers.

A binturong has rotating ankles...

... so it can swivel its feet around and climb
down trees headfirst hanging from its claws.

BEAVERS

Why does a beaver chomp through trees?

A North American beaver gnaws through trees and uses the wood to build a floating house called a lodge in the middle of a river. It also builds a dam in front of the house to stop it from washing away.

Inside a beaver's house ...

... there are two rooms, one for drying off and one bedroom filled with soft dry grass. There is a little hole in the ceiling to let in fresh air.

Did you know ...

... a beaver has see-through eyelids that it uses like swimming goggles?

A beaver has orange teeth ...

... because they contain orange iron. This makes them strong enough to cut down trees.

A multi-purpose tail

A beaver can use its tail to steer in the water and sit upright. A beaver hits its tail on the water to tell other, "Danger is coming!"

CHEETAHS

How speedy is a cheetah?

Cheetahs are the fastest animal on land and can go as fast as a car. After 30 seconds they get too hot and have to stop.

A cheetah is the only cat that can ...

... turn in mid-air. It swings its long tail to help it turn.

How does a cheetah run so fast?

A cheetah has claws that it uses like spiked running shoes. They help it to grip the ground when running.

PROWLING THE SUB-SAHARAN GRASSLANDS

A cheetah looks like it has been crying ...

... but it hasn't! A cheetah's black tear stripes make bright sun less dazzling.

Keep up cubs!

A cub is well camouflaged. A cub follows the bright white tip of its mom's tail to make sure it doesn't get lost in the long grass.

41

HONEY BADGERS

How did the honey badger get its name?

A honey badger's real name is a ratel. It gets its nickname because it is black and white like a badger and its favorite food is honey.

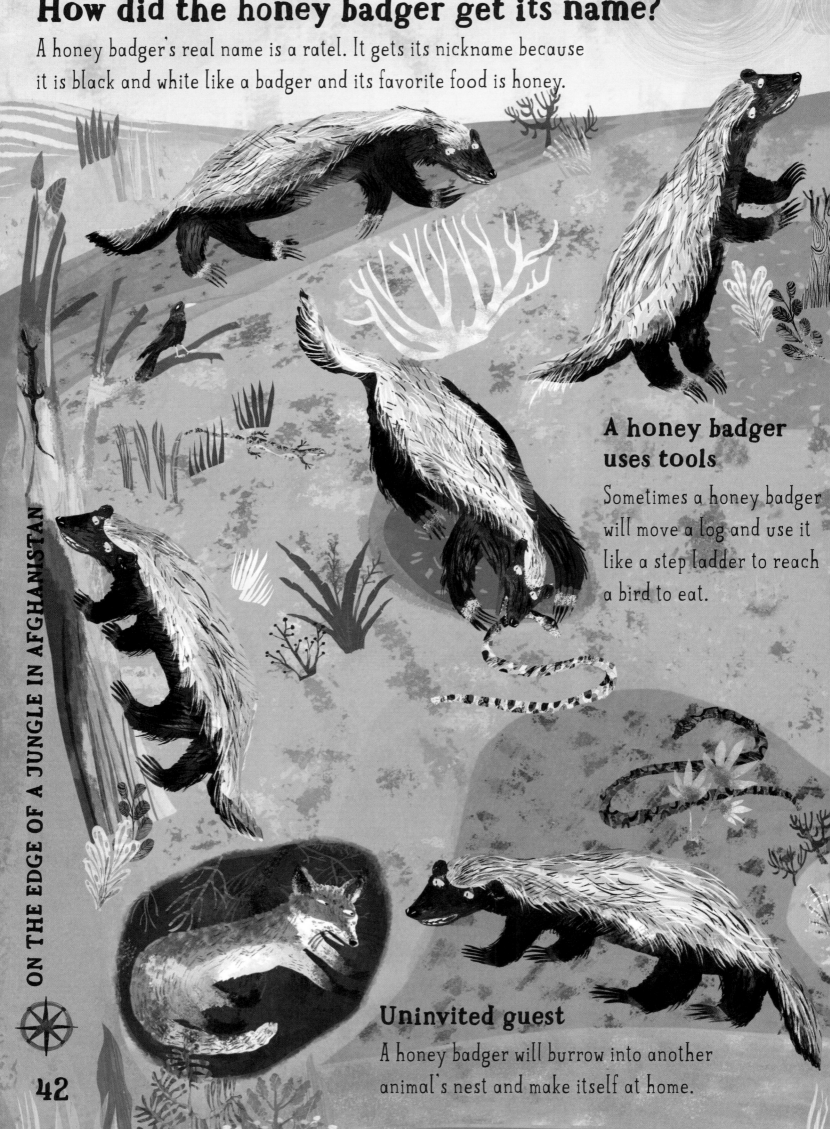

A honey badger uses tools

Sometimes a honey badger will move a log and use it like a step ladder to reach a bird to eat.

Uninvited guest

A honey badger will burrow into another animal's nest and make itself at home.

Partners in crime

A honey badger works together with a honeyguide bird to track down a bees' nest. When they find one, they share the honey inside.

What a stink!

A honey badger makes a liquid that is so smelly, it can hypnotize a nest of bees. While the bees are stunned, the honey badger eats all of their honey.

Thick-skinned

Thick fur and skin protect a honey badger from bee stings and snakebites.

WARTHOGS

How warty is a warthog?

Warthogs have big lumps on their faces called warts. They are like cushions that protect a warthog's face in a fight.

Trusty tusks

A warthog uses its four sharp tusks for lots of different things. It uses them as dangerous weapons but also as tools to rummage around for food.

A warthog kneels down to eat

When it is hungry, a warthog kneels down on its padded knees to eat grass.

Piglets run around in single file

Each piglet follows the tufty tail of the one in front so that it doesn't get lost.

Helpful friends

A warthog often lets birds ride on its back. The birds help the warthog by pecking off the insects that tickle its skin.

PORCUPINES

Why are porcupines spiky?

A porcupine is covered in big sharp spikes called quills. A porcupine puffs up its quills to protect it from other animals that might try to eat it.

A newborn porcupine has soft quills

Its quills become hard after a few days so it can defend itself.

Charge!

A porcupine charges backwards into its enemies. It can also rattle its quills to scare predators away.

SNUFFLING AROUND A CANADIAN FOREST FLOOR

A porcupine never goes bald

When a porcupine spikes its enemies, its quills come out. But a porcupine won't ever run out of quills because it can grow new ones.

A porcupine's home ...

... is called a den. A porcupine will make its den in hollow logs or even under houses!

47

HIPPOPOTAMUSES

Why do hippos love the mud?

Because it keeps them nice and cool. Hippos spend 18 hours a day in the water but can't swim!

WALLOWING IN A SUB-SAHARAN SWAMP

Angry, angry hippos

A hippo is one of the most aggressive creatures in the world. It has huge front teeth called tusks that it uses to fight other hippos. A hippo loves to yawn and show off its tusks as a warning.

Hippo suncream

A hippo makes its own suncream. It sweats out a sticky red liquid that protects it from the hot sun.

Flying poo

The main male hippo in the family flings his poo in the air to mark his territory.

Did you know ...

... a hippo's closest-living relatives are whales and dolphins?

49

BEASTLY FOOTPRINTS

ICE AGE BEASTS

What happened to the Ice Age beasts?

Ice Age beasts died out over 10,000 years ago when the world warmed up and cavemen started hunting them. We know what they would have looked like from cave paintings and fossils.

Dire wolf

The dire wolf was much bigger than the modern wolf. Its short legs meant that it could not run very fast, but it was vicious and strong.

Giant short-faced bear

At 12 feet tall, this bear was twice the size of the biggest bears alive today. It is the biggest meat-eating mammal ever to have lived on the planet!

Ground sloth

The Ice Age ground sloth was much too heavy to climb trees. It was as big as the giant short-faced bear but only ate leaves.

Saber-toothed cat

This giant cat had two front teeth the length of daggers. It used its terrifying teeth to hunt bison and other big beasts.

Woolly mammoth

A woolly mammoth would have been the same size as an African elephant. It had fur that was 3 feet long and enormous long tusks.

SAVE THE BEAST!

Which beasts are in trouble and why?

Some beasts are dying out because humans are damaging their natural habitats. Sometimes beasts are hunted for special body parts that humans want to use in traditional medicines or for decorations. Here are some of the most magnificent beasts in the greatest danger, and the things people are doing to save them.

Orangutan

The rainforests that an orangutan would normally call home are being chopped down to grow cooking-oil plants. Orphanages look after babies who have lost their homes. They are released into the wild once they have grown up.

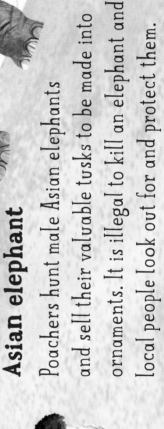

Asian elephant

Poachers hunt male Asian elephants and sell their valuable tusks to be made into ornaments. It is illegal to kill an elephant and local people look out for and protect them.

Giant panda

Pandas live in China and love to eat bamboo. Forests where the bamboo grows are being cut down to make room for houses and roads. Many pandas now live in zoos and sanctuaries.

Tiger

Farmers kill tigers to protect their animals from being eaten. As people move closer to the jungles where tigers live, they are hunted more and more. Some tigers now live in safe reserves where there are no people at all.

Sumatran rhino

Sumatran rhinos are hunted for their horns. The ground-up horns are used in some types of traditional medicine. Hunting rhinos has now been made illegal.

Iberian lynx

An Iberian lynx has to watch out for speeding cars as they often get run over. People are working hard to make lynx habitats safer and their numbers are growing every year.

BEASTS ON YOUR STREET

Why do wild animals come to town?

There is always food in our trash cans and often it is much warmer in the city than the countryside. There are also lots of places to shelter and fewer other animals to hunt them. Here are some of the most common city slickers from around the world.

Red foxes

Red foxes can be found in cities **all over the world**. They love to tip over our bins and rummage for food. Sometimes they travel up to town just for a snack, and then go home again.

Baboons

In **South Africa** lots of baboon habitats have been destroyed. Sometimes a baboon must come into town to find food and shelter. A baboon is very brave and naughty and sometimes steals shopping bags full of food straight out of people's hands!

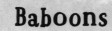

Brushtail possums

In **Australia**, a brushtail possum scurries around the city on power lines. A possum's favorite city snacks are the nuts and seeds from birdfeeders.

Racoons

The **North American** city racoon is very crafty. It can use its little hands to open tin cans and makes its home in warm chimneys.

Black bears

The black bear causes havoc in some **North American** towns. They are clever, super strong and can break through car doors to find food.

DID YOU FIND...

... all the things from the "Can you find?" questions and the 15 mystery footprints from the beginning of the book?

16–17 Baboons

8–9 Claws and jaws

18–19 Bats

12–13 Armadillos

24–25 Wolves

14–15 Foxes

26–27 Brown Bears

30-31 Lions

34-35 Hyenas

36-37 Binturongs

42-43 Honey Badgers

46-47 Porcupines

48-49 Hippopotamuses

52-53 Ice-age beasts

54-55 Save the beast!

BEASTLY WORDS

How to talk like a beast expert

Here are some words to use when you talk about beasts.

Beastly bodies
A beast is what we call a wild **mammal**. A mammal has warm blood, hair or fur on its body and a female gives birth to live babies, instead of laying eggs.

The place that an animal chooses to live is called its **habitat**. Some mammals **hibernate** which means they sleep through the coldest months.

A mammal is a **vertebrate**, which means it has a backbone. It has hard bones inside its body which make up an **endoskeleton**.

What does a beast eat?

All living things have their own place in the **food chain**. Their place in the food chain is decided by what they eat and what eats them.

A **carnivore** eats other animals and is at the top of the food chain. If it catches its own food it is a **predator**, but if it eats leftovers it is called a **scavenger**.

An **omnivore** eats both plants and animals.

A **herbivore** eats only plants, and is low down the food chain. It is hunted by other animals as **prey**.

INDEX

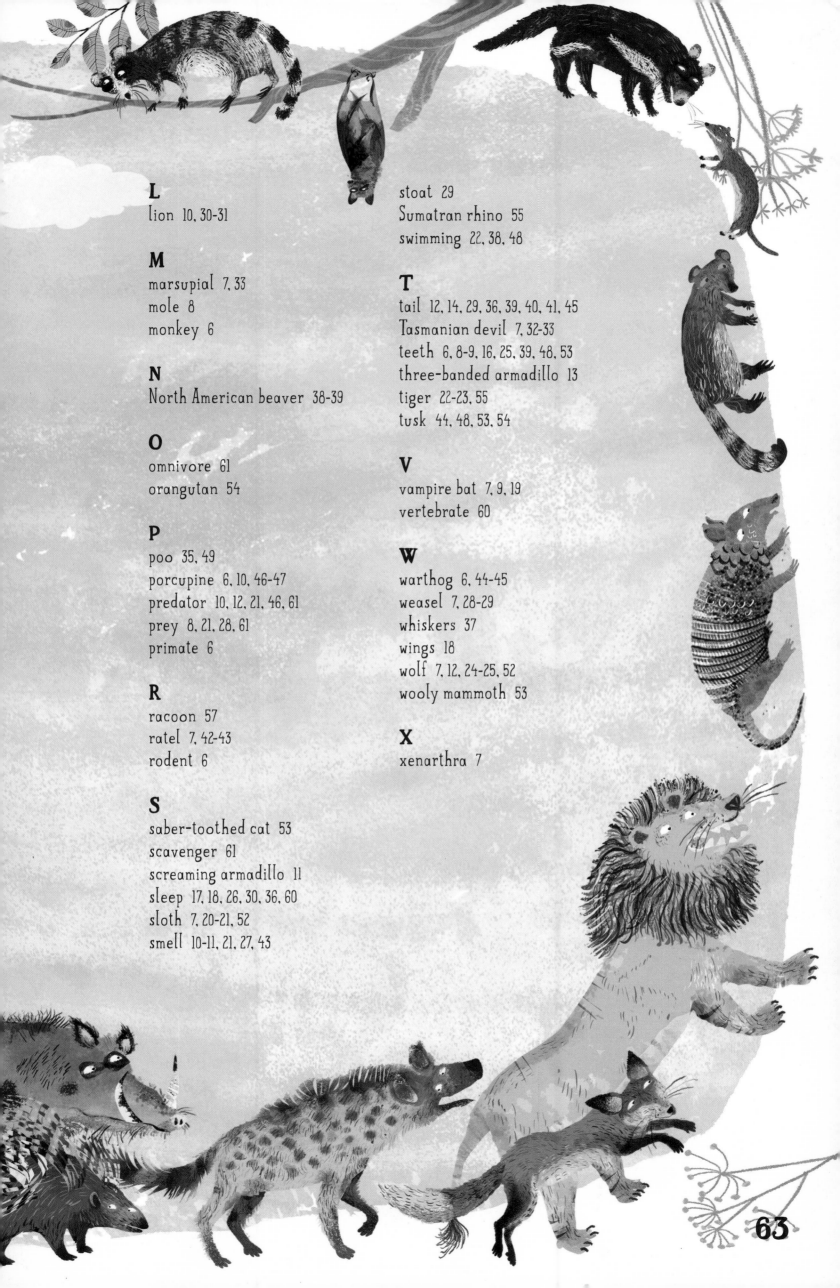

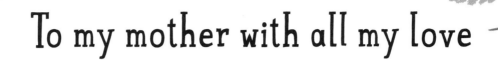

To my mother with all my love

Big beastly hugs and thanks to my editor Lucy Brownridge and my designer Aaron Hayden

The Big Book of Beasts © 2017 Yuval Zommer

First published in 2017 in the United States of America by Thames & Hudson Inc., 500 Fifth Avenue, New York, New York 1011

www.thamesandhudsonusa.com

Library of Congress Catalog Card Number 2016943103

ISBN 978-0-500-65106-3

Printed and bound in China by Reliance Printing (Shen Zhen) Co., Ltd.